POWER

INTERVIEWING

PROVEN JOB INTERVIEW TECHNIQUES THAT GET YOU RESULTS!

ORESTE J. D'AVERSA

PUBLISHER'S NOTE

This book is designed to provide accurate and authoritative. Information in regard to the subject matter covered. It is sold with the understanding that neither the author nor publisher is engaged in rendering psychological, legal or other professional service. If psychological, legal, professional advice or other expert assistance is required, the services of a professional, in that field, should be sought. The principles and concepts presented in this book are the opinions of the author and based on his interpretations of the aforementioned principles. Neither the author nor publisher is liable or responsible to any person or entity for any errors contained on this book, website, or for any special, incidental, or consequential damage caused or alleged to be caused directly or indirectly by the information contained on this book or website. Any application of the techniques, ideas and suggestions in this book is at the reader's sole discretion and risk.

FIRST EDITION

ISBN: 978-1-952294-09-9

Published by: Cutting Edge Technology Publishing.

TABLE OF CONTENTS

1. About the Author...5

2. Introduction...7

3. The Interview Process 9

4. Types of Interviews... 11

5. Delivering Your Accomplishments............................. 17

6. The Five Most Important Interview Questions.................23

7. Practice! Practice! Practice!...................................27

8. Before the Interview 29

9. During the Interview 33

10. After the Interview...37

11. Conclusion.. 41

12. More Interview Questions 43

NOTES

ABOUT THE AUTHOR

Oreste J. D'Aversa is a Job Search Coach and has worked with hundreds of people to help them find new and better jobs. Delivering real world experience as a former Executive Recruiter and Human Resources Manager.

Mr. D'Aversa is also business owner, Business Coach, Consultant, Trainer, Author, Public Speaker, University Lecturer and Advisor to Senior Management, providing Strategic Planning, Consulting and Training services to, Small Businesses, Entrepreneurs, Salespeople and other Consultants.

He has appeared on radio and television to discussing his books on professional and personal development.

He is author of the following books:

- *The Resume Writing Kit*
- *SELLING for NON-SELLING Professionals*
- *SELL More Technology NOW! Proven Sales Methods and Established Practices that Deliver Results*
- *Life Beyond The Pandemic: A Practical New Journey Handbook*
- *(all available on Amazon.com).*

He can be reached at:
Oreste J. D'Aversa, Owner
Metropolitan Small Business Coaching LLC
www.MetroSmallBusinessCoaching.com
eMail:OresteDAversa@outlook.com

NOTES

2. INTRODUCTION

The Interview...the deciding factor on whether or not you get the job. You are being judged, against the company's standards and against other candidates who are applying for the same position. Whatever your situation, you can be sure of being subjected to anywhere from one to several interviews before securing your next position.

We will be discussing the following topics:

- **The Interview Process** – Most companies have a certain methodology in interviewing candidates.

- **Types of Interviews** – Companies use different types of interviews to either "screen you in" or "screen you out" as a candidate for consideration.

- **Delivering Your Accomplishments** – Companies want to know about your results in past employment situations.

- **The Five Most Important Interview Questions** – Learn how to answer these important interview questions like a professional.

- **Practice! Practice! Practice!** - The pros practice and so should you!

- **Before the Interview** – Know what you should be doing before the interview.

- **During the Interview** – Know what you should be doing during the interview.

- **After the Interview** – Know what you should be doing after the interview.

- **More Interview Questions** – Some more interview questions to help better prepare you.

This book is meant to be a guide to help you prepare for your interviews. Follow the information and exercises and you will find yourself confident and well equipped to handle the interviews you secure. For some, this book may be filled with new information; for others a refresher course to brush up on your interview skills.

Regardless of your situation, this book will help you win more jobs by being better prepared and mastering the skill of interviewing.

3. THE INTERVIEW PROCESS

Be prepared for anything from a telephone interview by a third party (someone who does not work directly for the employer) to multiple in-person interviews, by a panel of people, with the Human Resources department, your next boss, your future peers, future subordinates, high level executives, and even the President and CEO of the company. Furthermore, the interview process does not necessarily have to go in any specific order. In one company you may meet the President first in another company you may meet with the President last or not at all.

It is import that you understand that interviewing is indeed a process; a process that may not always make sense to you but it does to the employer. A process in which you may or may not be kept informed about your progress, within that process, or the results of that process. At times it will sound confusing. Other times it will make no sense at all. Yet other times it will go like clockwork. Regardless of the mechanics of the process, your role is to be prepared and give a good interview whether or not you are offered the position.

Interviewing is both an art and a science. The science part is easy, knowing what questions to ask, from both your employer and yourself, while the art part is a bit more of a challenge. Any time you deal with people, things are never "black and white".

Your future employer is trying to find out basically three things with the interview process (and for that matter so should you!).

1. **General Questions** – Basic questions that would be asked at any interview.

   - Tell me about yourself.

   - What do you know about our company?

2. **Questions About Your Skills** – Questions about your specific skills, accomplishments, and abilities. Basically, can you do the job?

   - Tell me about a work accomplishment and why is it important.

   - Give an example where you used your skills to solve a problem

3. **Will You Fit into The Company** – Questions about where you will fit into the corporate culture. Do not underestimate this area. You may be qualified for a position but if your future employer feels you may not fit into the company's culture you will not be hired.

   - Tell me about your management style.

   - How would you describe your personality?

Remember one very important thing; the interview process is what you can do for the company - not what the company can do for you. It is all about the company while you are interviewing. It becomes all about you when you get the job offer!

4. TYPES OF INTERVIEWS

There are various types of interviews being conducted in the marketplace. Each type of interview has its own purpose. There is no one right interview method or one type of specific set of interview questions that are better or worse than another.

In this section you will learn about the various types of interviews. In your travels you will probably come across other types of interviews as well. It all boils down to which one your future employer feels has merit as a tool to screen potential candidates. Keep an open mind and understand that the main purpose of the interview is just a tool to help the employer with the selection process.

In any interview process answer truthfully, try to relax and just be yourself.

1. Structured versus Unstructured Interviews

Most companies use a structured interview method when interviewing candidates. A structured interview has a beginning, middle and an end. The structured interview also ensures employers that they are in compliance with fair employment practices and other rules and regulations as prescribed by law.

Usually, the **structured interview** will have a predetermined set of questions and a trained interviewer has been given a specific amount of time to perform the interview. A structured interview may have the following format:

1. Greeting with some small talk

2. Introduction

3. Work Experience

4. Additional Skills

5. Discussion of strengths and weaknesses

6. Description of position

7. Candidate (your) questions

8. Close

The structured interview is designed to learn as much as possible about the candidate's qualifications for the position.

Unstructured interviews are more casual and tend not to have any direction. Sometimes, the interviewer is not trained in interviewing or may have been asked to interview you at the last moment.

These types of interviews can be frustrating because it appears that there is no clear purpose or direction in the questioning process. Should this happen it is important to try to lead the interview without dominating the conversation. Remember that every interview should be a process about learning about the company. So take this opportunity to learn something that is of value to you in your decision making process.

2.   Pre-Screening Interview

More and more companies are using a pre-screening interview before an actual live face-to-face interview. Understand that is a "real" interview and you should be just as prepared as a face-to-face interview.

The purpose of this interview is to see if you meet the basic criteria of the position. Does your criterion match the employer's criteria? How do you present yourself on the phone? Questions here tend to be short, concise and to the point. This interview may be performed by: a third party company, an executive recruiter, a company recruiter, human resources personnel which may include the human resources executive (manager or vice president), your future boss, his boss or the president of the company. Rest assured that this is a real interview and its purpose is to either "screen you in" for a face-to-face interview or "screen you out" so they can move on to the next candidate.

3.   Third Party Screening Interview

There will be times when an employer will choose to use a third party (someone who is not part of their company). Just because it is a third party does not mean it is any less important. The employer has chosen to work with a third party for any number of reasons, one of which could be using an executive recruiter, that is, a firm who specializes in this type of employee placement. Another example would be an employee screening firm that uses tests or a series of specially designed questions to perform the pre-screening for the employer.

Remember, these people are being paid by your future employer to select "the best" candidates for their clients. Treat them with respect and courtesy. While they cannot hire you, they do make the decision as to whether you are selected for consideration in advance in the hiring process.

4. Team Interviews

There may be times when you will be interviewed by members of a team all at the same time. This is done for a number of different reasons. One reason is to see how to act in a group situation. If you are in sales, for example, you may be performing group presentations. A team interview will give your future employer an insight on how you handle yourself in a professional situation.

Another reason is that it allows the employer to have more of their current employees involved in the interview process. Help move the selection process along. An employer may make Friday interview day. With this method interviews can be conducted quickly and efficiently.

If an employer designates a certain day for interviews be prepared for a day of sequential interviews. This means a morning or even a full day of interviews. You may be meeting with members of the team on an individual basis and they, in turn, are interviewing people all day as well.

Also, the team or panel interview demonstrates to your future employer how you handle a stressful situation. Aside from your qualifications and skills it gives the employer some insight into your behavior. Some companies use behavioral interviews to see how you perform, handle yourself or "act" in a given situation.

NOTES

5. Delivering Your Accomplishments

Employers hire people who can perform skilled tasks for them. Your future employer is extremely interested in your professional accomplishments. You have accomplished work objectives in the past; chances are that you will be a strong contributor to your new employer in the future. You want to demonstrate to the person conducting the interview that you played an active role in your career and were not a spectator who watched from the sidelines.

Look at the following statement and choose the stronger word. "Assisted" the Human Resources Department in writing the employee handbook", OR "Collaborated" with the Human Resources Department in writing the employee handbook". Assisted sounds like you supplied paper for the copy machine while Collaborated infers you were working shoulder to shoulder with Human Resources Department to create the employee handbook.

The following list of verbs, which by no means is complete, is a good place to start your search for strong action verbs/words to describe what you have accomplished.

Adapted	Designed	Investigated	Protected
Advised	Developed	Judged	Questioned
Administered	Diagnosed	Learned	Read
Analyzed	Directed	Lectured	Reasoned

Applied	Discovered	Led	Recommended
Approved	Displayed	Listened	Reconciled
Arranged	Drew	Located	Recorded
Assembled	Edited	Maintained	Recruited
Assessed	Encouraged	Managed	Reduced
Assisted	Estimated	Measured	Reinforced
Balanced	Established	Mediated	Reorganized
Budgeted	Evaluated	Memorized	Repaired
Classified	Expedited	Mentored	Reported
Clarified	Followed	Monitored	Researched
Coached	Forged	Motivate	Restored
Collected	Formulated	Negotiated	Retrieved
Coordinated	Founded	Nurtured	Revised
Communicated	Gathered	Observed	Reviewed
Compared	Generated	Operated	Scheduled
Compiled	Guided	Organized	Shaped
Completed	Handled	Originated	Simplified
Computed	Helped	Participated	Solved
Conceived	Identified	Perceived	Spoke
Conceptualized	Implemented	Performed	Synthesized
Conducted	Improved	Persisted	Streamlined
Confronted	Improvised	Persuaded	Studied

Constructed	Increased	Planned	Supervised
Contrasted	Influenced	Prepared	Supported
Controlled	Initiated	Presented	Taught
Coordinated	Integrated	Processed	Tested
Comprehended	Inspired	Produced	Trained
Counseled	Installed	Programmed	Treated
Created	Instructed	Promoted	Tutored
Decided	Interpreted	Proposed	Validated
Defined	Interviewed	Proved	Volunteered
Demonstrated	Invented	Provided	Wrote

OARS – Objective/Action/Result/Statement

It's all about accomplishments. What have you done for your employers?

The OARS formula will help you describe to the reader your professional accomplishments.

O - The business **OBJECTIVE** (problem, challenge, etc.) for which you were responsible to perform.

A - The **ACTION** you took to solve the business objective usually begins with an ACTION VERB (See section).

R - What was the **RESULT** that you obtained measured in some type of quantifiable terms. For example, saved or made a company money, saved time, increased productivity, reduced costs, etc.

S - The **STATEMENT** is what you put together from the above three items.

OARS Accomplishment:

Objective + Action + Result = Statement

The following OARS Statements are examples from Resumes. You can communicate these same statements in your interview in a more conversational manner. Good OAR Statements use action verbs. The order is not as important as to all items (Objective/Action/Result) are identified.

1. Increased sales through new prospects and installed base accounts, expanding sales by 30%.

2. Created and conducted interview training program for managers reducing candidate interview process by 25%.

3.   Implemented an order processing system which increased efficiency in the customer service department when interfacing with clients.

NOTES

6. THE FIVE MOST IMPORTANT INTERVIEW QUESTIONS

While all interview questions are important, the following questions set the tone for the interview, and you should have the answers to all of these questions prepared.

1. Tell me about yourself.

At face value this seems like an easy question but do not be fooled. What the interviewer wants to know about you in a brief 60 to 90 second overview is the following information:

a. High level discussion on your work histor

b. Educational background

c. Current Situation

d. Future

The answer is about you as a professional and not about your personal life.

2. What do you know about our company?

Based on your research, you should be able to give some summary level information about the company. You would have gathered this information from the company website or research you performed in the business section of the library such as information about the company's history, products, services or the people within the organization.

3.   What were the most significant business accomplishments you made in your last job?

If you recall, in a previous section of this manual there was a discussion of your accomplishments. Be prepared to talk about those accomplishments in your interview.   The interviewer wants to know how you made a difference for past employers. Having made a difference for your previous employers, chances are very good that you will make a positive difference for this employer. This will help set you apart from other candidates that you are competing against for this position.

4.   What are your strengths/weaknesses?

Mention two or three of your key strengths with some examples. Try to tie these strengths to the position you are applying for or research you have performed about the company. For example, you have strong software package implementation skills. Your research shows that the company just purchased a new software package that needs to be implemented in the next 6 months.

For your weaknesses, offer only one and mention what you have learned from that weakness and how you changed your behavior as a result.

5.   Why should we hire you?

This question, whether asked or not asked, is always in the mind of the interviewer. You should be striving to answer this question whenever the opportunity presents itself. Even if it means you saying, when the time is right, "I would make a good hire because ...", and cite past work experience to the current position, relative accomplishments and any skills that would benefit the company.

In summary they should hire you because you will save them money, make them money, reduce costs, increase productivity and you will have a positive impact on their bottom line. You are an asset not a liability, bringing value to your future employer.

NOTES

7. PRACTICE! PRACTICE! PRACTICE!

Interviewing, like any other skill, needs to be learned, practiced and mastered. There cannot be enough emphasis on this matter. Maybe you haven't interviewed in many years or are not sure what may be asked of you. Why take a chance? You need to be prepared. Though the interview can be a stressful situation you can manage that stress by being prepared. There is no substitute for practice and preparation.

How do you practice for an interview?

There are several methods you can use to practice for an interview:

1. Read interview questions out loud to yourself and answer them as you would in an actual interview situation. The purpose of this exercise is to get you familiar with the interviewer's question and answer process and for you to rehearse your answers. It will also help make you feel comfortable with the types of questions that might be asked of you.

2. Practice your interview questions by using a tape recorder and then play the recording back to you. Give honest feedback to yourself. Do you have a verbal "tic" such as "hmm" or "ya know"? Are you positive and upbeat or do you sound like a "sad sack"? You will be able to hear yourself as the interviewer actually does and

make the appropriate changes to your answers and speaking before you have your interview.

3. Practice interviewing using a video camera. Video yourself or have someone else film you and observe you both visually and orally. How are you sitting? How is your tone and rate of speech? You will actually see yourself in action in a controlled environment. Remember - a picture is worth a thousand words! You will be amazed with what you will learn about yourself using this technique.

4. Practice interviewing with your friends, family or associates.
    Explain to them that they should take this exercise seriously and you want them to give you meaningful feedback to improve your interviewing skills; not to be critical but rather to offer feedback on how you can improve your skills.

Work with a career search professional. A career search professional has been trained and has performed many interviews. You would be receiving professional training and coaching from someone whose job is interviewing. You get your income taxes prepared by a professional, so why not learn interviewing skills from a professional.

8. BEFORE THE INTERVIEW

L ike a professional athlete who needs to prepare for the next game, you too must prepare for your next interview. Preparation takes many forms and there will be an examination of some things you should be doing before the interview.

1. Company Research

You need to research the company before you meet with them. Research can be performed using the internet, in the business reference section of your public library or, if possible, someone who you know is currently working for the company. The company will expect you to be knowledgeable about the goods and/or services they provide. Summary level information about the company is fine. It demonstrates to the company that you are well prepared and if you are well prepared for your interview chances are that you will be well prepared for the job you are seeking. It would be a very big strike against you if you have not performed some basic research about your company, especially in this day and age. With the advent of the internet, there should be no excuse for the lack of preparation on your part.

2. Prepare Interview Questions

You should be interviewing your prospective employer while the employer is interviewing you. You should prepare questions in writing, to bring with you and ask (when appropriate) about the company, position and compensation. Some sample questions are: What are the challenges you currently face in the marketplace? What type of individual are you looking for to fill this position? Questions about compensation are better left when you feel you are a finalist for the position. Usually, the prospective employer will start the conversation about the compensation package. Have your questions ready when the time is right. An interview is a dialogue not a monologue, so it is perfectly logical for you to have questions for the interviewer.

3. The Interview Kit

Informally known as "The Interview Kit" these items are necessities when going for an interview: Extra copies of your resume, your professional references, your interview questions, a sample of your work as to "leave behind" (if applicable), a clean briefcase or portfolio. Sometimes your resume may get lost and the interviewer will require a copy or you will be interviewing with people who have been called in at the last minute to interview and they do not have a copy of your resume. Always be prepared, because you never know who you might meet in your interviews.

4. Manage Pre-Interview Stress

You can manage pre-interview stress with a host of various exercises. One thing is to go over your research about the company the day before the interview. Practice your interview questions and answers, especially the questions you feel the most uncomfortable talking about. Talk to others about your interview and ask if they have any suggestions about your preparation. Take a walk to clear your mind and get a good night sleep the day before your interview. You want to be well rested and refreshed on the day of your interview. These suggestions should help you manage your pre-interview stress in a productive manner.

5. Dress for Success

It is very important that you manage your image in the interview. A company hires the "whole package" when they hire you; not just your intelligence but also you as a person. Look the part that you want to be hired for. For most office positions, a business suit is still the standard attire for an interview. Forget dressing down for now. If that is the corporate culture you will be told and then you can dress accordingly. No extremes in clothing, jewelry or anything else for that matter. Dress conservatively and look professional. Everything should be neat and clean about you from your head to your shoes.

6. Get Directions and On Time

One of the worse things you can do in an interview is to be late. The world has become a much busier place today. Time is money. Get directions, leave ample travel time and definitely be on time. The internet has become a popular method of getting directions but be careful; the directions are not always accurate and do not take into consideration road construction, traffic, accident and so on. If necessary, take a practice run a day or two before the interview. Better yet, do the practice run at the same time you would be going for the interview. We all know that traffic at rush hour is much different that traffic off-peak. Remember, excuses do not go over well. It is your responsibility to be there on time. I cannot stress this enough.

9. DURING THE INTERVIEW

The big day is finally here. You have prepared and practiced. It is time for the face-to-face interview!

While you are Waiting

If you are asked to wait in a reception area for a few minutes before your interview, that would be the time to notice your surroundings. As you are being judged as to your appearance, you too should be judging the company on its appearance. Is the office clean and well kept, are the people happy or does everyone look sad, mad or unhappy to be there? Are there awards on the walls, articles about the company displayed, company information you can read while you are waiting? Is this an environment that will help you grow and prosper as an employee and individual?

Try To Relax and Be Yourself

Although an interview may be a stressful situation try to relax and be yourself. It is important to make a good first impression with the interviewer. Build rapport and smile; it helps you connect with your interviewer in a positive manner. Be mindful of your body language. One technique in the use of body language is to "mirror" the interviewer's body language. If they sit up straight you sit up straight and so on. Let the interviewer set the agenda of the meeting and listen carefully to his/her questions. Take a moment to think your answers through before you say them. The interview is an information gathering process and not an interrogation so both parties should be calm and levelheaded. The company has shown some interest in your abilities or you would not be there in the first place.

Ask Questions

When appropriate, ask questions to better understand the companies concerns or point-of-view. It is perfectly acceptable to take notes and have a written set of questions with you during the interview process. You should ask questions when necessary and appropriate to get a better understanding of the topic or to learn more about a given subject. If your questions are not answered during one or more interviews, make sure they get answered before you accept the job. You should not have any open questions before you accept the position.

Remember an interview should be a dialogue between the two parties. Take your cues from the interviewer. Some interviewer will want you to do most of the talking and they do most of the listening. Other interviewers will be the opposite. Still other interviewers will be in the middle.

Sell Yourself with Your Accomplishments

Always try to deliver your accomplishments while you are interviewing. The "so what" factor plays an important part during the interview process. You will answer a question posed to you by an interviewer and in his/her mind they're saying to themselves "so what", "what's the big deal"? The way you eliminate the "so what" factor is with your accomplishment statements. Your accomplishment statements tell the listener how you made the difference in that particular situation. If you made a positive difference with your former employer, chances are good that you will have a positive impact with your new employer. Interviewers like to see that in a candidate. That is one way you separate yourself from other candidates.

As the company is selling you on how good the company is, you should be selling them on the value of your contributions with the use of your accomplishment statements.

Concluding the Interview

If you felt the interview went well and you are speaking with whom you feel is the hiring authority don't be afraid to say things like: "I feel I can do this job and would like to be a part of your team. What are the next steps in the hiring process?" This will demonstrate your enthusiasm to your employer. Other questions you can ask are: "When can I follow up with you to discuss the results of today's interview?" or "What's your opinion on how things went today?" The more you interview the more comfortable you will be asking these types of questions.

NOTES

10. AFTER THE INTERVIEW

Thank You Letters

After the interview, or series of interviews, make sure to send everyone a thank you letter. It is extremely important that you send a thank you letter within 24 to 48 of the interviews. In the letter, you want to thank the interviewer for their time, mention some accomplishments and how you can contribute to the organization. Lastly, ask for the job!

You may want to send the letters via email and also a hard copy letter through the mail. The impact of email is immediate then the letter will show up in a few days. This way you can be "in front" of the interviewer without being a nuisance.

Critique Yourself

After the interview, take a few minutes to perform some post-interview analysis on your performance during the interview process. Be honest with yourself for this exercise:

Were you prepared properly? Did you speak too rapidly?

What went well?

What did not go so well?

What interview skills need improvement? Was I a good listener?

Did I ask enough questions and were they appropriate questions? Did I bond and establish rapport with the interviewer?

You should be learning with every interview and getting more proficient with your interview skills.

Handling Rejection

Unfortunately, rejection is a part of the interview process. It is important not to take this rejection personally. I know it is easier said than done. That is why you need to have a mechanism to handle your rejection.

Perhaps you can talk to someone about your interviews. Exercise or meditation is a constructive means to deal with the rejection. Then let it go and prepare for your next interview. As sure as the sun rises there will be other opportunities in the marketplace.

Handling Offers

Conversely be prepared to handle job offers that will be extended to you; the result of all of your work and preparation – the job offer. It is an exciting time to receive an offer from your future employer. It is perfectly acceptable to take 24 to 48 hours to consider the offer and discuss it with your family and other professionals. Make sure that the offer is in writing and covers everything you discussed with your future employer.

Always Be Positive

Interviewing can be demanding and be a real roller coaster ride on your emotions. Keep things in proper perspective in your job search. Stay positive; balance your job search with proper nutrition, stress management, family, and friends.

Remember that it is a numbers game the more interviews you participate in the closer you get to a job offer.

NOTES

11. CONCLUSION

You now have information on how to prepare for an employment interview. You have learned about the various parts of the interview process from the process itself to preparing and articulating your accomplishments, to what you need to know before, during and after an interview.

There cannot be enough emphasis on practicing your interviewing skills. Interviewing like any other skill, needs to be learned, practiced and mastered. Practice by yourself, with friends or family or go on networking meetings with business associates. If need be work, with an interviewing professional; someone with experience who can coach you and make you more effective.

You will find the more interviews you participate in the more comfortable you will be with the interviewing process and the more comfortable you will be with others and yourself. Another tip is to keep scheduling interviews until you receive and accept an offer from an employer.

Now go out there and interview like a professional and get the job of your dreams!

NOTES

12. MORE INTERVIEW QUESTIONS

Below are some more sample questions that may be asked in the interview process. The list is by no means complete but should give you some insight as to what might be asked.

Remember, always keep your answers positive and when appropriate use your accomplishments to demonstrate the value you can bring to your potential employer.

1. Why do you want to work for us?

2. Why do you want to leave your present job?

3. What can you offer our company that someone cannot?

4. What do you like/dislike about this position?

5. What do you look for in a position?

6. What are your expectations out of this position and our company?

7. What is your management/supervisory style?

8. How would you describe your personality?

9. What is important to you when you hire someone?

10. Have you ever had to terminate someone's employment? How did you handle the situation?

11. What do you find is the most difficult thing about being a senior executive/manager/staff member?

12. What did you like most/least in your last/current position?

13. What has been your greatest professional challenge?

14. How do you get along with your former boss?

15. How do you handle criticism?

16. How do you work under pressure?

17. Where do you see yourself in our company in five years?

18. What does success mean to you?

19. How do you stay current in your industry?

20. Why are you currently unemployed?

21. Describe your computer skills.

22. What are your salary requirements?

23. How quickly can you contribute to our company?

24. What kinds of decisions are difficult for you?

25. What can I tell you about our organization?

NOTES

NOTES

* 9 7 8 1 9 5 2 2 9 4 0 9 9 *